SAMPLE ENTREPRENEURSHIP PROJECT PROPOSAL AND BUSINESS PLAN FOR XYZ ECOTOURISM FARM: A GUIDE BOOK FOR COLLEGE STUDENTS FINAL PROJECT

P.O. BOX 1

ACHUT AYIENG
Tel:
Ph.:
Fax:

BY: AUGUSTINE AFULLO

ISBN-13: 978-1517179632

ISBN-10: 1517179637

AUGUSTINE AFULLO
CO-PUBLISHED BY
1. WAMRA TWECHNOPRISES, P.O. BOX 36665-00200, NAIROBI, KENYA +254722690956
2. CREATE-SPACE, USA

Printed by AMAZON, USA

First published 2015 Set in Sylfaen 10/12

ISBN-13: 978-1517179632

ISBN-10: 1517179637

DEDICATION
This book is dedicated to all Students undertaking an entrepreneurship based course across the world, for herein lies the answer to all unemployment.

About The Author:

Professor Augustine Afullo is an environmental health consultant, manager and trainer. He holds a doctoral (PhD) degree in Environmental science, a Master of Science degree in water and environmental management (MSc-WEM), a Master of Philosophy degree in Environmental Health (MPhil- Environmental health) and a Bachelor of Science degree in Agriculture (BSc Agric). Augustine has professional post-graduate qualifications in health education, environmental science, education and professional certificate qualifications in occupational safety and health (OSH) (chartered institute of environmental health (CIEH-UK)), research methods (RSA) and landscaping, ornamentals and lawn management (BCA, Botswana). Professor Afullo is a former Assistant professor in the North Central College, Naperville, Illinois, USA. He is an alumnus of the Fulbright Scholar in Residence (SIR) and commonwealth association alumni. He is also an associate member of the African Waste and Environment Management Centre (AWEMAC), a National Environment and Management (NEMA- Kenya) registered and licensed lead expert in environmental assessment, a registered trainer in the chartered institute of environmental health (CIEH-UK), a former member of the chartered institute of water and environmental management (UK), and the African studies association (ASA). Augustine has over 20 years of teaching, capacity building, training, lecturing and research experience in environmental management, water, sanitation, and hygiene (WASH) in Eastern, Southern Africa and the United States of America. He has done many environmental impact assessments, monitoring and evaluation (M&E) tasks as the lead consultant, and supervised at least forty post graduate (advanced diploma, Masters and doctoral) students. Dr Afullo has published widely in refereed environment, occupational health, sanitation, hygiene, water, food and nutritional security and public health journals. Augustine is currently a reviewer of a number of academic journals as well as a member of the advisory board of the world research journal of environment and waste management. He is ken on using the environment for entrepreneurship.

Contents

1.0   Preamble

This proposal outlines the vision, mission, and strategies for the proposed XYZ ECOTOURISM farm project (XYZE). XYZE is meant to be a private game farm in which undomesticated animals are kept for a wide range of purposes. The project proposes to construct a number of physical structures. When completed, its projected annual budget will be about 197,000 US$. It intends to start with a US$ 480,000 bank loan proposed to be paid from the end of the fifth year of its establishment. This will be paid over duration of 5-7 years, depending on the agreement with the loaning institution. Our projected breakeven period is 5 years upon launching.

1.1   Our Vision

XYZE's vision is to conserve. Conservation is the sustainable utilisation of nature and natural resources. Sustainability means using natural resources in such ways that they would be able to maintain their populations in perpetuity; including balancing of species that share the same habitat. This means maintaining species diversity in suitable habitats with self-sustaining populations in order to utilise such species.

1.2   Mission statement:

We strive to provide a perfect environment for photographic safaris, recreation, game shooting / trophy hunting, attraction, and learning with a sound basis for eco-tourism.

2.0   INTRODUCTION

Game farming is the intensive management of game animals. Game animals are undomesticated fauna often termed as wildlife.

2.1   Importance of Game

Game farming is important in a number of ways. These are:

a.   Source of income;

b.   Source of game meat;

c.   Conservation of endangered species;

d.   A recreational facility;

e.   Research promotion;

f.   Widens use of non-arable land;

g.   Creation of employment.

It is therefore imperative that game farming should be promoted where it is possible and appropriate. Tanzania is a case in point.

2.2   Tanzania: Facts.

Tanzania's economy mainly comprises 5 sectors. These are: agriculture, forestry and fishing (50%; electricity, gas and water (20%); services (12%); Transport, storage and communications (6%); and manufacturing (6%). The rest of the sectors contributing to gross domestic product (GDP) are almost negligible.

The country is more than 50% medium and high agricultural potential, receiving at least 750 mm/annum. The northern part bordering Lake Victoria is the driest, extending north-eastwards to the coast. The southern half of the coastal region is high potential, with the northern half being low potential. The low potential areas receive less than 750 mm/annum, with the average being 500 mm. This is still good enough for dry land crops, but is even better for wildlife. This is where game farming comes in. July is the driest month throughout the country, whereas January is the wettest month. Temperatures

2.3   Project justification.

Tanzania has a land area of 883,663 km^2, a population of about 40 million, a population density of close to 30 persons/km^2, and an annual population growth rate of about 3.0%. About 40%

% of Tanzania is arid or semi-arid. Most of the land fall within the Zone 3-8 of the United States Department of Agriculture (USDA) land classes, rendering them non-arable. At best, they can only be used for grazing, tree planting, or wildlife management. Unfortunately, at the moment, most arid and semi-arid lands are considered by the majority of the Tanzanians as wasteland. We want to demonstrate that all land is a valuable resource. Secondly, XYZ ECOTOURISMis a historically important ancient town.

2.4 Game parks, game reserves and other tourist attractions in Tanzania

There are at least five major national parks in Tanzania. These are Serengeti (North), Katavi (Western), Ruaha (South-central), Mikumi (Eastern), and Moshi (North eastern). There are also another six game reserves. These are: Rungwa ((Central-south); Ugalla (Central-west); Biharamulo (southern shores of lake Victoria, north west); Selous (South east) Mkomazi (eastern), and Ngorongoro (Northern). Key tourist centres are: Arusha, Moshi, Zanzibar, Tanga, and Daressalam; key prehistoric sites are Kondoa and Ol duvai; while historic sites are Isimila and Songomara island. Recreational fishing is done along the Indian Ocean shores, especially Zanzibar and Daressalam.

2.5 Proposed project location

We propose to be based at midway point between Daressalaam and Bagamoyo. Looking at the distribution of major recreational sites, the Dar- XYZ ECOTOURISMarea has very little tourism attraction spots. Yet many tourists commonly visit Dar on transit to other places within the country, especially the game parks and game reserves. Dar has a population of close to 3 million, rendering it a good market for local and international tourism. This is why it would be worthwhile establishing a wildlife attraction spot close to Dar to maximise on tourist satisfaction. Our catchment will be 5 million residents within a radius of 150 km from our base, as well as international tourists.

FIG 1: MAP OF TANZANIA

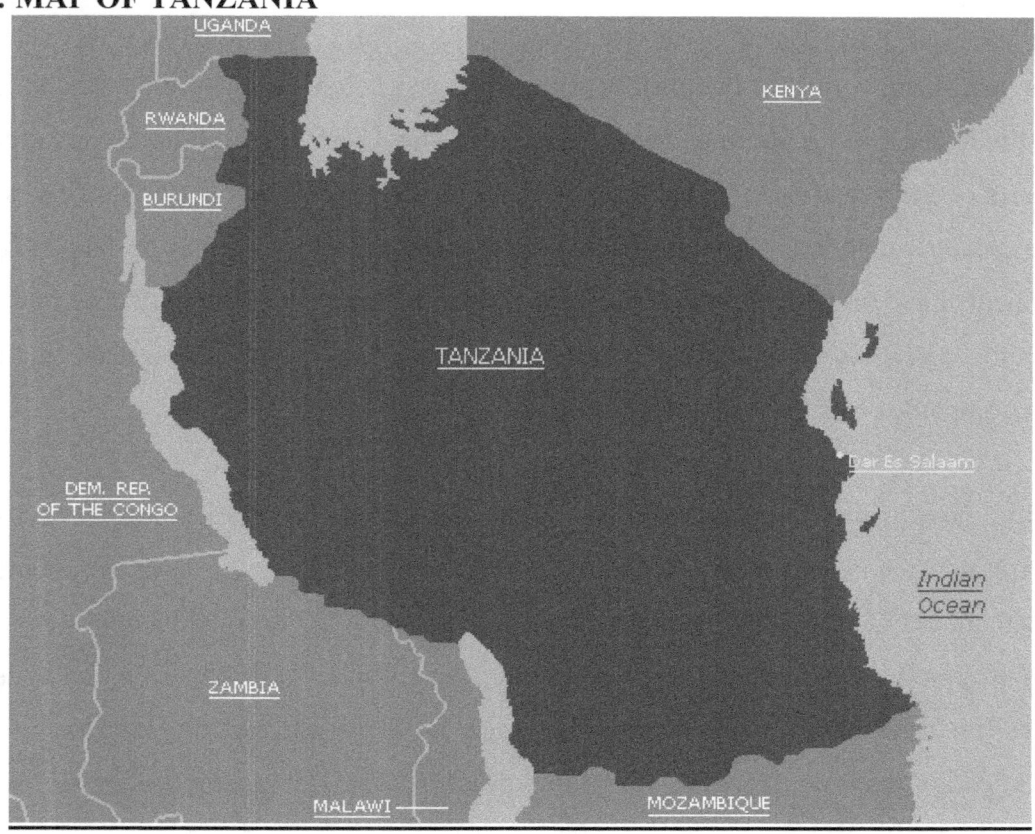

FIG 2: MAP OF PROPOSED LOCATION OF XYZ ECOTOURISM FARM

3.0 Concerns to be addressed

In Tanzania, the government owns most game parks and game reserves. Whereas this ensures and instils a sense of community ownership, many state-managed and owned institutions in most parts of the world have either deteriorated overtime or totally collapsed. This is due to insufficient operation and mentenance strategies, aspects which define sustainability. The governments have therefore lost both real and potential income by some potential tourists and / or visitors going to other countries where there are modern facilities. Tanzania's main tourism competitor has been South Africa.

Secondly, most of the Tanzania national game parks and game reserves are more than four decades old. Many have therefore become out-dated, and some tourists are not encouraged to visit, as there are no new and / or modern facilities. This has led to some level of deterioration of service. Yet the government has offered training to millions of Tanzanians in a wide range of fields. It is time these young beneficiaries of the tax-payers money dug back some of their knowledge and income into this very important revenue-generating sector to help the government create employment and get more income.

3.1 Existing Opportunities and strengths we intend to exploit

We hope that as private operators in this vital sector, we will demonstrate and utilise effectively the following advantages:

1   Game farms have low management option than cattle ranches as it is less labour intensive;
2   Comparative advantage whereby due to specialisation, we can offer more competitive and better services than institutions that handle a wide range of activities and offer diverse services such as the government;
3   Less bureaucracy, due to the simpler nature of the private enterprise;
4   Availability of loans for investment by the citizen-owned private enterprises;
5   Regional integration, with the broader East African market opening up for more business;
6   Tanzania's membership of the SADC is bound to give more chances to SADC based private entrepreneurs as well;

7   A new socio-economic mood in the region with renewed commitment of the leaders to peace, as is the case with Angola, Rwanda and Burundi;

8   The establishment of the African Union (AU) and its twin outfit, NEPAD, whose focus is economic as opposed to its predecessor, the OAU whose focus was political liberation.

3.2   TABLE 1: SWOT ANALYSIS

INTERNAL SITUATION	EXTERNAL SITUATION
STRENGTHS	**OPPORTUNITIES**
1. Strong professional background of proprietors. 2. Strong advisory and management team. 3. A one-stop game farm 4. Diversification; 5. Affordable package for local tourists; 6. One of the newest in the market- making tourists curious; 7. Availability of modern facilities 8. Increasing demand for game meat	1. Available loaning facilities in the country 2. Wide and open market within Eastern Africa (especially with the EAC operational) 3. Strategic location (proximity to Dar and a major historically significant town, Bagamoyo) 4. Good and favourable road network. 5. Sparse population at the project area; 6. Favourable government policy on land acquisition 7. Available cheap labour in the region 8. Technical skills available in the region 9. Low management demands by game farms compared to livestock ranches. 10. Tanzania's dual membership of both SADC and EAC
WEAKNESSES	**THREATS**
1. Not initially intending to include big 5 in the first few years 2. High capital cost of investment 3. Inexperience in handling projects of this magnitude.	1. Competition from other game farms 2. High cost of the big 5 (major attraction) 4. High interest rates on loan. 5. Terrorism threats in the region 6. Diseases from wildlife entering the farm from outside 7. Negative publicity from animal rights organisations;

3.3 Project objectives

1. To conserve the endangered species of game animals;
2. To improve the living conditions of the animals;
3. To offer opportunities for game sports;
4. To diversify the economy of the Republic of Tanzania;
5. To conserve the local unique features and landscapes;
6. To improve the degraded lands by landscaping;
7. To offer the tourists, locals and other visitors a wider choice for recreation and entertainment;
8. To offer better international tourist understanding of the rural communities through cultural tourism;
9. To offer learning and training opportunities to the local and international community;
10. To offer employment to the Citizens;
11. To further the research in wildlife;
12. To reduce poverty
13. To contribute to community service by establishing social amenities such as schools, dispensaries.

4.0 PLANNED APPROACH AND ACTIVITIES

4.1 Development plan

Major physical structures will be established in phases. There will be up to 5 phases of development, each comprising 2 years. After every phase, there will be an evaluation, while monitoring will be an on-going process from the onset. The following sections give a brief outline of the proposed development plan. A table gives the same items in a summary form.

4.2 Land Acquisition

Acquisition of land of at least 10,000 hectares between XYZ ECOTOURISM and Dar-es-salaam will be the first thing. An initial 12 km X 12 km land is proposed. This will be followed up through the ministries of lands, and wildlife. Then environmental impact assessment (EIA) of the planned project will be conducted, so that all possible short and long term repercussions of the project are addresses before any further progress. Here, aspects such as community compensation and partnership will be negotiated. It is at this stage that the structure of the proposed partnership centre will be formulated. Land survey, boundary demarcation, and water survey will follow immediately.

4.3   Construction work:
The following will be the key physical structures for construction:

1.   Game-proof fence to 2.5 metres tall. This caters for even fence-defying wildlife such as elephants.

2.   Water and sanitation facilities construction (hardware), including boreholes, piping, septic tanks, sewerage, waste stabilisation ponds etc.

3.   The apiary, aviary, Snake Park, fish pond, frog pond, campsite and dams for game drinking and viewing.

4.   50 room capacity lodge and a campsite of 300 people capacity.

5.   Water tunnel with splash pool for children riding and other games.

6.   Roads for vehicle passage and nature trails for walking.

7.   20 chalets and 20 caravans to partly reflect and reinforce our cultural tourism objective.

8.   Multi-purpose hall complete with conference facilities, capable of hosting 3 conferences simultaneously. This will be for hire.

9.   Bar and restaurant where most game meat will be sold.

10.   Park and Botanical garden for conservation and recreation respectively.

11.   Research laboratory where analyses such as feed, assay and microbiological samples will be studied. Feed analysis will be done largely by proximate method. This will help in maximizing feed utilisation and disease control among the game.

4.4   Establishment of zoos
Establishment of zoos for snakes, cheetahs, zebras, tortoise, hyenas, Springbok, Impalas, Dikdik, Blesbok, Deer, Eland, Kudu, Gemsbok, Black wildebeest, wild pigs, chimpanzees, gorillas, bees, birds, Red hartebeest, Eland Female, Nyala, Waterbuck, Lion and Giraffe.

4.5   Game Purchase
We will purchase a wide range of game (as in item 4.4 above) and keep them in a 12 km X 12 km (14,400 hectares) game farm. Regional game auctions will be the main source of game for

stocking. We will initially concentrate on easy-to maintain, less water-dependant species. Therefore we will initially avoid the big 5 as Lion & leopard defy fences, while the rhinos are very expensive. They will be purchased during the project progress, as we accumulate enough disposable income before we start paying back the loan. We are optimistic that we will make some savings and get more income than projected, as we have generally assumed worst-case scenario in our planning, construction, account management and revenue projections. Some cheap game will be bought from the community members – as they hunt from their assigned areas during the official legal hunting season. We will also target low price seasons at auctions in Eastern and Southern Africa. We will initially focus on easy-to-manage game. This will guarantee us an early revenue. The programme is as follows (see also Section 23, table 15):

(i)   Months 1-6:   Impalas, Kudus, Eland, Zebra, Reedbuck, Blesbok, the zoo game etc(ref table 15)

(ii)   Months 6-12:   Giraffe, and increase numbers of Eland and Blesbok and other small game as per table 15.

(iii)   Yr 2   Bigger game

NB Buffalo and Blue wildebeest carry high risk of corridor disease and malignant catarrhal fever (snotsiekte) respectively. So they will be avoided.

4.6   Training:

This will focus on game capture and handling skills. Game will be captured for treatment, branding, transfer to a zoo or any other desired point. We will use outfitters where possible and appropriate to conduct our training sessions. (Outfitters are people licensed to trade internationally and must be qualified professional hunters). For professional hunter training, we intend to spare 450-600 US$ / course of 10-12 days to the majority of our personnel. The policy will be: Each personnel in the game farm should have some elementary training in professional game management and hunting. This will improve our capability. We will also offer the training to other prospective professional hunters using our trained personnel's' hands-on-experience, especially during low seasons. Since professional hunters are officially expected to get accreditation to a professional hunters' school, our training institution will serve that role for our personnel. Extending the membership to others outside our institution will earn us an income, as membership is renewable annually.

4.7   Other Purchases

10 Boats for boat rides, 10 tents for use in the campsite, five 4-wheel drive vehicles, 20 caravans, photographic equipment, office furniture and equipments.

5.0   Other Planned activities

5.1   Zoological Research:

We hope to embark on intensive zoological research with a view to both conserving our endangered and unique game, as well as to share with the community and the global community knowledge about wildlife. In this regard, we will form partnership with like-minded institutions so as to broaden our learning and training boundaries. We will strive to employ largely members of the host community with a view to harnessing their knowledge about wildlife so that this folk knowledge is documented. We will use both our internal revenue and externally sourced research funds. The latter will be done by writing research proposals.

5.2 Ordinary surveillance

Surveillance of game will be done to monitor their general condition, disease outbreaks and food situation assessment. This will be reinforced by veterinary services. XYZE will employ a full time veterinarian.

5.3 Cultural tourism:

This will be our focus since we realise that most tourists visit the developing world to have a true picture of the village (African) lifestyle. We will negotiate and link up with some villages to be our partners in this respect. This agreement will be reached during the land acquisition deal stage through a memorandum of understanding (MOU).

5.4 Environmental conservation:

We will strive to rejuvenate degraded lands and eroded soils with a view to recovering their productivity. In relation to this, we will establish a nature trail to help pedestrian visitors also visit the place, as in the past, game viewing has been like a preserve of only the rich tourists with posh and powerful four-wheel drive vehicles.

5.5 Landscaping and other environmental rejuvenation and beautification services.

All forms of landscaping shall be done. Both plant and non-plant materials shall be used. These include: water in waterfronts; rockeries, bricks, stones, flowers, shrubs, ground covers and lawn.

5.6 Documentation and resource centre:

This will serve as a library equivalent, though it will also have other facilities like computers for game management research and training. All on-going research and project work will be documented here. It will be open to all registered members and partners.

5.7　Sales and Marketing:

Marketing will be done using a wide range of methods- both modern and ancient to reach as many potential clients as possible. These are outlined in the work programme table. However, sale of game meat and other products will be done through the restaurant. After year 6, will use one of the international hunting conventions such as Safari Club international (SCI) or Dallas safari to increase the quality of tourists, which can increase to as much as USD 60$ / person / fortnight.

5.8 Auctions:

We will utilise modern technologies to market our available game for shooting to earn game trophies. We will use an external agent to do the booking of international professional hunters. There will be a professional hunter as our full time employee to guide our clients.

5.9 Establishment of a partnership centre.

This will focus on opening up and bringing together members of the centre at both institutional and individual basis. There will be membership fee payable depending on category. The host communities will be automatic partners and will not pay any membership fee, but individuals even from the same communities will need to pay for membership at individual category should they feel like. The structure for the centre will be a simple community- built house depicting all characteristics of the host community. The activities of this centre will be closely intertwined with those of the research laboratory, as well as those of the documentation and resource centre.

5.10 Energy policy:

We will use environmentally friendly solar systems such as the solar canteen. This will help save our energy needs and minimise our running costs.

6.0   TABLE 2: PHASED WORK PROGRAMME

PHASE	I		II		III		IV		V		OTHER
YEAR	▨	▨	3	4	5	6	7	8	9	0	11
EIA & EA	█			▒							▒
Market Survey	█										
General survey	█										
Market research	█	█	█	█	█	█	█	█	█	█	█
Boundary demarcation & clearing)	█										
Apiary construction	█										
Botanical garden	█	█	▒								
Nature trail	█	█	▒			█					
Lodges	█	█	▒								
Tents for campsite	█	█	▒								
Campsite	█										
Swimming pools	█	█	▒						█		
Aviary construction	█										
Zoo construction	█				▒						
Dams (Game drinking)	█	█	█		▒						
Snake park construction	█				▒						
Resource centre		█	█	█							
Frog ponds	█										
Golf course									█	█	
Fish ponds	█				█				█		
Game proof fence	▒		█								
Research laboratories			█	█							
Ordinary surveillance		█	█	█	█	█	█	█	█	█	█
Conference Complex	█	█									
Conference facilities	█	█	▒	▒							
Borehole drilling	█										
Tents10@600$	█										
Water distribution	█	█	▒	▒							
Caravan	█	▒									
Water reservoirs	█	█	▒						█	█	█
Recreational Park	█	█	▒								
Water tunnel (with splash pool)		█	█						▒		
Purchase of wildlife	█	█	▒	█							
Road Network	█	▒	▒	▒							
Solar canteen (cooking) (@ 1400$/80pple)	█		█		█						
Photographic equipment	█	█	▒	▒							
Waste management	▒	▒	▒	▒	▒	▒	▒	▒	▒	▒	▒
Lighting / power supply	█										
MARKETING	█	█	█	█	█	█	█	█	█	█	█

Veterinary services												
Environmental conservation												
Staffing												
Vehicles (4 WD)												
General Mentenance												
Establishment / offices												
Project management												

LEGEND

	HIGH LEVEL / HEAVY INVESTMENT
	MEDIUM LEVEL / MODERATE INVESTMENT
	LOW LEVEL / LIGHT INVESTMENT
	GENERAL MENTENANCE ONLY
	EXPANSION PHASE (LOAN REPAYMENT COMPLETE)
	RELY PARTLY ON INCOME GENERATED TO OPERATE
	100% RELIANCE ON LOAN / CONSTRUCTION PHASE
	FULL TIME LOAN PAYMENT YEARS
	BREAKEVEN YEAR
	LOAN PAYMENT BEGINS

7.0 TABLE 3: PERSONNEL AND HUMAN RESOURCE PROJECTIONS

Level	Grade \ Year	1	2	3	4	5	6	7	8	9	10
Senior	General Manager	1	1	1	1	1	1	1	1	1	1
	Professional hunter	0	1	1	2	2	3	3	3	3	3
	Advisors	2	2	2	2	3	3	3	3	3	3
	Proprietor	1	1	1	1	1	1	1	1	1	1
SUBTOTAL		**4**	**5**	**5**	**6**	**7**	**8**	**8**	**8**	**8**	**8**
Middle	Trucker*		1	1	2	2	3	3	4	4	5
	Range manager		1	1	1	1	1	1	1	1	1
	Wildlife researcher		1	1	1	2	2	2	3	3	3
	Veterinary doctor		1	1	1	1	1	1	1	1	1
	Managers	**4**	**7**	**8**	**8**	**8**	**8**	**8**	**10**	**10**	**10**
	Accounts	1	1								
	Restaurant	1	2								
	Logistics	1	1								
	Accomodation		1								
	Health & Nutrition		1								
	Construction	1	1	1							
	Conservationist								2		
SUB-TOTAL		4	11	12	13	14	15	18	20	20	20
Low	Tour guides		1	2	3	4	7	7	7	8	8
	Secretaries		2	3	3	3	3	3	4	4	4
	Drivers		1	1	1	1	1	1	2	2	2
	Others*		2	3	4	5	6	7	8	9	10
SUBTOTAL		0	6	9	11	13	17	18	21	23	24
TOTAL		8	22	26	30	34	40	44	49	51	52

Notes:

1. Managers will be departmental heads.
2. Logistics manager will be in charge of Transport and partnership.
3. Extra personnel employed per year will depend on the existing situation.
4. Salary ratio of 2:3:5 for low, middle-level and high category personnel respectively will apply.
5. After 10 years, the project will have an employee population of 52 in the ratio of 8:20:24 for high, medium and low cadres respectively. The high cadre class will form

the top management team. Each member of this team will be in charge of a section and personnel about which he / she will report during the meetings.

6. The truckers will check boundary fence and keep an eye on illegal hunting (1 worker / 500 ha)

TABLE 4: FINANCES I: ESTIMATED COST OF ITEMS (in thousand US$)

ITEM	PROGRESSIVE ANNUAL EXPENDITURE (USD) (X 1000)										
YEAR	1	2	3	4	5	6	7	8	9	10	11
Land	2	-	-	-	-	-	-	-	-	-	-
EIA & EA	2	-	-	1	-	-	-	-	-	-	2
Survey	2	-	-	-	-	-	-	-	-	-	-
Boundary demarcation & clearing)	1.2	-	-	-	-	-	-	-	-	-	-
Apiary construction	0.5	-	-	-	1.0	-	-	-	-	-	-
Botanical garden	2	2	2	-	-	2	-	-	-	-	-
Nature trail	5	2	5	-	-	5.0	-	-	-	-	-
Lodges	50	50		-	-	-	-	-	-	-	-
Tents for campsite	2	2	2	2	-	-	-	-	-	-	-
Campsite	5	5	3	3	-	-	-	-	-	-	-
Swimming pools	2	2	2	-	-	-	-	-	10	-	-
Aviary construction	1.0	-	-	-	-	-	-	-	-	-	-
Zoo construction	2.0	-	-	-	1.5	-	-	-	-	-	-
Dams (Game drinking)	5	5	5	-	5	-	-	-	-	-	-
Snake park construction	1	-	-	-	1	-	-	-	-	-	-
Resource centre	-	5	2	-	-	-	-	-	-	-	-
Frog ponds	1.0	-	-	-	-	-	-	-	-	-	-
Golf course	-	-	-	-	-	-	-	-	10	10	-
Fish ponds	1.0	-	-	-	1.5	-	-	-	1.5	-	-
Game proof fence	25.0	25.0	-	-	-	-	-	-	-	-	-
Research laboratories	-	10	10	-	-	-	-	-	-	-	-
Ordinary surveillance	-	5	5	5	5	5	5	5	5	5	5
Market research	3.0	2.0	2.0	2.0	2.0	2.0	2.0	2.0	2.0	2.0	2.0
Conference Complex	30	20	-	-	-	-	-	-	-	-	-
Conference facilities	10	5	5	5		-	-	-	-	-	-
Borehole drilling	5.4	1.8	-	-	-	-	-	-	-	-	-
Tents10@600$	6	-	-	-	-	-	-	-	-	-	-
Water distribution	2	1	1	1	-	-	-	-	-	--	-
Caravan	2	4	2	-	-	-	-	-	-	-	-
Water reservoirs	1.0	1.0	1.0	-	-	-	-	-	2	2	2
Casual labour	1.0	5.0	5	5	5	5	1	1	1	1	1
Recreational Park	2	2	2	-	-	-	-	-	-	-	-
Water tunnel*	-	5	5	-	-	-	-	-	10	-	-
Purchase of wildlife	20	20	20	10	10	-	-	-	-	-	-
Road Network	10	5	5	5	-	-	-	-	-	-	-
Solar canteen (cooking) (@ 1400$/80pple)	2.8	-	3.2	-	3.5	-	-	-	-	-	-
Photographic equipment	5.0	1.0	1.0	1.0	1.0	1.0	1.0	1.0	1.0	1.0	1.0
Insurance	3	3	3	3	3	3	3	3	3	3	3
Waste management	2.0	2.0	2.0	2.0	2.0	2.0	2.0	2.0	2.0	2.0	2.0
Lighting / power supply	15	-	-	-	-	-	-	-	-	-	-
Marketing: Internet	1.0	1.0	1.0	1.0	1.0	1.0	1.0	1.0	1.0	1.0	1.0
Subscription	0.5	0.5	0.5	0.5	0.5	0.5	0.5	0.5	0.5	0.5	0.5
Print media	1.0	1.0	1.0	1.0	1.0	1.0	1.0	1.0	1.0	1.0	1.0
Tour agents	1.0	1.0	1.0	1.0	1.0	1.0	1.0	1.0	1.0	1.0	1.0
Brochures	1.0	0.1	0.5	0.1	0.6	0.2	0.7	0.1	0.5	0.1	0.5
Trade fairs	1.0	1.0	1.5	1.5	2.0	2.0	2.0	2.0	2.0	2.0	2.0
Business meals	1.0	1.0	1.0	1.0	1.5	1.5	1.5	1.5	2.0	2.0	2.0
Veterinary services	1.0	1.0	2.0	2.0	3.0	3.0	3.0	3.0	4.0	4.0	4.0

Item											
Env. onservation	1.0	1.0	1.0	1.0	1.0	1.5	2.0	2.0	2.0	2.0	2.0
Feeds	2	2	2	3	3	3	3	3	3	3	3
Staffing	10	15	20	25	30	35	40	40	40	40	40
Vehicles (4 WD)	20	-	30	-	30	-	-	-	15	15	-
Vehicle Spare parts	0.5	1.0	1.0	1.5	1.5	2.0	2.0	2.5	2.5	3.0	3.0
General Mentenance	0.5	2.0	2.5	2.5	3.0	3.0	3.5	3.0	4.0	4.5	5.0
Establishment / offices	20	2	2	-	-	-	-	3.0	3.0	4.0	-
Taxes	3	3	3	3	3	3	3	4	4	4	5
Project monitoring	1	1	1	1	1	1	1	1	2	2	2
Project evaluation	-	2	-	2	-	2	-	2	-	2	-
TRAINING	1	2	1	1	1	1	1	1	1	2	2
GAME RESEARCH	-	1	1	2	2	2	2	2	2	3	3
Miscallaneous	2	2	2	2	3	3	3	3	4	4	4
TOTAL (US$ X 1000)	296.4	232.9	168.2	97.1	130.6	91.7	85.2	90.6	142	126.1	99

9.0: REVENUE:

A table of revenue, with footnotes to explain the basis of the estimates, is given below.

9.1   TABLE 5:   FINANCES II: ESTIMATED REVENUE (in thousand US$)

Item		Year									
Item & annual income growth rate (%)		2	3	4	5	6	7	8	9	10	11
Aviary/ apiary	20	1	1.2	1.4	1.7	2.0	2.4	2..9	3	3	4
Nature trail	50	2	6	7	7	8	8	8	9	9	10
Lodge s(50)	40	5	45	63	88	90	90	90	90	135	150
Restaurant	20	1	1.2	1.4	1.7	2	2	2	3	3	4
Bar	25	1	1.3	1.6	2.0	2.5	2.5	3	3.2	3.2	3.5
Park	15	.4	.5	.6	.7	.8	1	1	1	1	1.2
MP 1Hall Hire	20	-	10	12	14	17	20	24	29	35	40
Vehicle Admission fee	50	1	1.5	2.3	3.4	5.0	5.0	5.0	5.5	6	6
Game 14meat	50	1	2	3	4.5	6.8	10.0	10.0	10.0	14	14
Water sports	25	2	10	13	16	20	25	25	30	30	30
Game Shooting *	10	-	30	33	36.3	40.0	44.0	48.4	52.4	55	60
Membership/ Gymn	20	.5	.6	.72	.86	1.0	1.2	1.4	1.7	2	2
Conferences	40	2	4	5.6	7.8	11	15	17	18	20	23
Campsite	50	5	7.5	11.2	16.8	17.0	17.0	18.0	18.0	20	23
Children park	25	-	5	6.3	8.0	10.0	10.	10.0	12.0	12	14
Game drives	25	10	13	16	20	25	31	40	40	50	55
Laboratory	10	.1	.25	.28	.31	.34	.37	.41	.41	.45	.5
Zoo & pool	15	5	12	14	16.1	18.5	21	21	23	25	25
Chalets (20)	25	8	10	13	16	20	25	31	40	40	45
Resource & doc centre	10	-	-	1	1.1	1.2	1.3	1.5	1.7	2	2
Tents accomodation	20	2	4	8	10	12	14	17	20	20	20
Photographic shooting	50	10	15	23	34	51	77	115	115	120	120
GROSS TOTAL ANNUAL INCOME (000 US$)		67	179	237	305	361	432	490	525	595	657

Notes

*See appendix I (year 2 uses)

(i) Lodges: 50 <u>rooms@50US$</u> at 150 days occupancy rate per year;

(ii) Multi-purpose (MP) / Conference Hall Hire: 180 days / <u>year@US$</u> 100

(iii) Campsite: 200 clients / <u>yr@US$</u> 5

(iv) Caravan: 5 used / night in 10 <u>nights/yr@30US$</u>

(v) Membership / Gymn: 20 members / yr @30US$

(xi) Water sports (water tunnel & boat drives): 3600 clients / yr@ USD 2

(xii) Laboratory service:

(xiii) Zoo & Pool: 3600 clients @ US$ 5

(xiv) Vehicle admission: 720 vehicles / yr@ US$ 5

(xv) Trophy sales & game shooting / hunting: 30 / yr@ US$1,100

(vi) Recreational Park:100 clients / yr@ USD5

(vii) Nature Trail walks: 3600 clients / yr @ USD 2

(viii) Game videos: 700 sold / yr@ 20US$

(ix) Educational Tours:24 / yr @ 10 US$

(x) Game rides: 3600 clients / yr@ US$ 10

(xvi) Tents accommodation: 200 clients / yr @ 50 US$ / client

(xvii) Chalets: 150 occupancy days / year @ 100 USD

(xviii) Values underlined and bolded are the take –off income levels after which there is steady income from the investment it represents;

(xix) % in column 2 are the projected annual increase in returns from each item.

10.0   HUNTING AND CITES REGULATIONS:

The main sources of income from this project will be (i) Meat for Venison and biltong (ii) Hides (iii) Hunting for trophies (iv) Tourism and   (v) selling excess game. Some fee is payable for sending the trophy overseas, and these trophies must have CITES permit even if the species is not on the endangered species list. For springbok, the permit will certify that the antelope is not a CITES species. Everything will be done to meet the CITES regulations.

10.1   SHOOTING & HUNTING POLICY AND TERMS OF PAYMENT

When a deal is struck with a potential hunter / shooter, the following will be the terms of payment: At least 50% deposit paid, then the remaining 50% paid before shooting; Game hunting to focus on Kudu* (currently the most sought for in RSA by international hunters). We will guard against captive bred or Canned lions. This is an immoral method of hunting where by an animal is shot from a close range or from the back of the vehicles while feeding on a bait. According to international hunting rules, an animal in captivity meant for hunting should be released at least 24 hours before the hunt, and the animal may not be hunted in a camp smaller than 1000 ha, and this area must be approved by the right department. Similarly, breeders may not permit hunting on the same farm. (Farmers weekly, pp 31, August 2002).

11.0   TABLE 6:   FINANCE III (a): GROSS AND DISCOUNTED INCOME PROJECTIONS, AND MARGINAL RATE OF RETURN (MRR) (IN 000 US$)

PHASE	1		II		III		IV		V	
Year	1	2	3	4	5	6	7	8	9	10
Total Gross annual income	-	67	179	237	305	361	432	490	525	595
DISCOUNTED marginal INCOME / YEAR ** (A)	-	54.4	131	156	181	193	208	213	206	210
MARGINAL COSTS / YEAR (B)	296	233	168	97.1	131	91.7	85.2	90.6	142	126
Marginal Rate of Return (MRR = A/B) in %	-	23.3	78.0	161	138	210	244	235	145	167

Notes:

(i)   ** Computed at 11% annual discount rate (the higher side of the market bank rates of 8-11%; worst case scenario).

(ii)   The Current development bank loans go for an interest of 14.75 (prime rate) plus 2-4%. This gives a range of 16.75 - 18.75%. Since the intended loan is payable within 5-7 years, the higher side, assuming the worst-case scenario, will be adopted. Thus using an annual interest rate of 18.75%, the marginal rate of return (MRR) to investment exceeds the bank interest rate. We therefore feel that the loan is worth it since from the time we start getting an income from the investment, the MRR (23.3%) exceeds the market interest rate (18.75%).

12.0   TABLE 7: FINANCE III (b): GROSS TOTAL INCOME PROJECTIONS, TOTAL ANNUAL / MARGINAL EXPENDITURE AND MARGINAL RATE OF RETURN (MRR) (IN %)

END OF YEAR	0	1	2	3	4	5
Interest (i) (000 US$)		90	107	127	151	204
Expenditure (E) (000 US$)	296	233	168	97	131	92
TOTAL ANNUAL EXPENDITURE / MARGINAL EXPENDITURE (a)	296	323	275	224	282	296
Undiscounted net income (b)	-	-	67	179	237	305
MRR (b/a)	-	-	24.4	79.9	84.0	-
Bank interest rate	11	11	11	11	11	11
Comment	-	-	Invest	Invest	Invest	Invest

13.0 TABLE 8: FINANCE IV : NET INCOME PROJECTIONS, NET WORTH OF BUSINESS, AND FINANCIAL STABILITY OF PROJECT (IN 000 US$)

PHASE	1		II		III		IV		V	
Year	1	2	3	4	5	6	7	8	9	10
Total Gross annual income (A)	0	67	179	237	305	361	432	490	525	595
MARGINAL COSTS / YEAR (B)	296	233	168	97.1	131	91.7	85.2	90.6	142	126
NET GROSS ANNUAL INCOME (A-B)	-296	-166	+11	+14	174	269	347	399	383	469
CUMMULATIVE ANNUAL INCOME	-296	-462	-451	-437	-263	6	353	752	1135	1604
NET DISCOUNTED ANNUAL INCOME(***)	-296	-135	+8.0	+9.2	103	144	167	173	150	165
CUMMULATIVE NET DISCOUNTED ANNUAL INCOME	-296	-431	-423	-414	-311	-167	0	173	323	488

** Computed at 11% annual discount rate (the higher side of the market bank rates of 8-11%; worst case scenario); *** The discount rate used is 11% p.a.

14.0 TABLE 9: FINANCE V: SENSITIVITY ANALYSIS (AMOUNT OF LOAN REQUESTED) (3 Significant figures)

LOAN (000 US$) (A)	BALANCE PUT IN ACCOUNT TO EARN INTEREST YEAR 1 (B)	INTEREST EARNED YEAR 1 © (10% OF B)	TOTAL FUNDS AVAILABLE FOR YEAR 2 (Add yr 2 revenue)***	CUMMULATIVE LOAN PAYABLE AT END OF YEAR					
				1(D)	2(E)	3(F)	4(G)	5(H)	NET TOTAL LOAN PAYABLE (H-C)
530	227	22.7	250 (304)	629	747	888	1054	1252	**1229**
500	204	20.4	224 (279)	594	705	837	994	1181	1160
498	202	20.2	222 (277)	591	702	834	990	1176	1155
495	199	19.9	219 (273)	589	699	831	986	1171	1151
490	194	19.4	213 (268)	582	691	821	974	1157	1138
485	189	18.9	208 (262)	576	684	812	964	1143	1124
480	184	18.4	202 (257)	570	676	802	953	1131	1113
476	180	18.0	198 (252)	565	671	797	947	1124	1106
463	167	16.7	184 (238)	550	653	775	921	1093	1077
462	166	16.6	183 (237)	550	652	774	919	1091	1074

*** Minimum Amount of funds needed is 233 + (10% reserve) for use in Yr 2 development = 256.3 (256 in 3 sf)

(i)   Lowest prevailing savings bank interest rate is 8%; rage is 8-11%; worst case scenario would have been assumed, but It is assumed the call account will offer more than the minimum ordinary saving account interest rates. Thus the expected interest rate on the savings for year 1 is 10%. Thus C = B X 0.1

(ii)   (B) is the difference between A and the year 1 cost of 296,400 USD (ie, B=A-296)

(iii) Annual Interest Rate for development Loan = 14.75 % + 4%= 18.75% (Rates range from 14.57%   prime rate + 2-4% pa)

(iv)   530 is the total capital requirements for years 1 and 2;

(v)   500 is the maximum ceiling the borrower has set;

(vi)   The portion of the loan not spent in year 1 (B) will be placed in a call account in a bank.

(vii) Conclusion: Will need 480,000 USD. Anything less can stall the project. Anything more will earn unwarranted interest on the loan, leading to less profit margin.

15.0   TABLE 10: FINANCE VI: PAYMENT SCHEDULE (7- year payment plan)

OPTION I: PAYMENT SCHEDULE AT END OF YEARS 5-11 (In 000 US$) (4 sf)

END OF YEAR	0	1	2	3	4	5	6	7	8	9	10	11
Net cumulative Loan payable (Capital + interest)	480	570	675.5	802.1	952.5	1131	1179	1137	1001	783.7	551.8	183
Loan less interest							993.1	957.4	842.9	660.0	464.7	153.8
Undiscounted net income	-	-	67	179	237	305	361	432	490	525	595	657
EXPENDITURE						131	92	86	91	142	126	99
Reserve Balance in Account*	-	-	-	-	-	42	47	52	58	64	71	79
TOTAL IN ACCOUNT						173	139	138	149	206	197	178
LOAN PAID	0	0	0	0	0	138	222	294	341	319	398	183

Notes:
*Keep a balance of 25,000 USD discounted equivalent per year. 25,000 US$ (in current value) expressed in their future equivalents in different years, using a discounting rate of 18.75%. (Balance after paying loan Equivalent to the current 25,000 US$)

16.0   TABLE 11: FINANCE VII(a) : PAYMENT SCHEDULE (5- year payment plan)
OPTION II: PAYMENT SCHEDULE AT END OF YEARS 5-10 (In 000 US$) (4 sf)

END OF YEAR	0	1	2	3	4	5	6	7	8	9	10	11
Net cumulative Loan Balance payable (Capital + interest)	480	570	675.5	802.1	952.5	1131.1	1166	1095	919.3	647.5	343.8	0
Cummulative Loan less interest	-	480	570	675.5	802.1	952.5	982.5	922.2	774.1	545.3	289.5	0
Undiscounted net income	-	-	67	179	237	305	361	432	490	525	595	657
EXPENDITURE		296	233	168	97	131	92	86	91	142	126	99
Reserve Balance in Account	-	202**	36***	47****	187*****	25	25	25	25	25	25	25
TOTAL IN ACCOUNT		202	36	47	187	156	117	111	116	167	151	124
LOAN repayment CAPABILITY	0	0	0	0	0	149	244	321	374	358	444	533
LOAN PAID	0	0	0	0	0	149	244	321	374	358	344	0

(i)   **NOTES:**   Keep a balance of US$ 25,000 discounted equivalent per year during the loan payment period (Years 5-10)

(ii)   *25,000 US$ (in future value) for emergency situations eg court cases, compensation etc.

(iii)   ** Balance of unspent loan (184) placed in a call account and earns 10% interest, gives 202.4 at end of yr 1.

(iv)   *** 31 is taken from the revenue of year 2 (67) to top up the deficit, and tops up the net available funds (202) to give the net expenditure of 233 for the year. Thus the net untouched / saved revenue at end of year 2 thus becomes 36.

(v)   ****47 = 36(saved the previous year) plus net income (11) during year 3 (179-168)

(vi)   *****: 187= previous year's savings (47) + net savings during   year 4 (237-97=140);

(vii)   Assumption: **Annual Interest rate on development loan = 18.75% p.a. (Compound)**

17.0   TABLE 12: FINANCE VII (b): PAYMENT SCHEDULE (5- year payment plan) OPTION II: PAYMENT SCHEDULE AT END OF YEARS 5-10 (In 000 US$) FIGURES COMPUTED TO THE PRESENT VALUE EQUIVALENTS (DISCOUNTED) USING 11% interest rate.

END OF YEAR	0	1	2	3	4	5	6	7	8	9	10	11
Net cumulative Loan Balance payable (Capital + interest)	480	518	548	587	610	671	624	527	399	253	122	0
Cumulative Loan less interest	-	437	463	494	528	565	525	444	336	213	102	0
Discounted net income	-	-	54	131	156	181	193	208	213	206	210	209
EXPENDITURE		269	189	123	64	78	49	41	40	55	44	31
Reserve Balance in Account	-	184**	29***	35****	123*****	15	14	12	11	9.8	8.8	7.9
TOTAL IN ACCOUNT		184	29	35	123	93	63	53	51	65	53	39
LOAN CAPABILITY	0	0	0	0	0	88	130	155	162	141	157	170
LOAN PAID	0	0	0	0	0	88	130	155	162	141	122	0

NOTES:

(i)   Keep a balance of 25,000 US$ Discounted equivalent per year during the loan payment period (Years 5-10)

(ii)   *25,000 US$ (in future value) for emergency situations eg court cases, compensation etc.

(iii)   ** Balance of unspent loan (184) placed in a call account and earns 10% interest, gives 202.4 at end of yr 1.

(iv)   *** 31 is taken from the revenue of year 2 (67) to top up the deficit, and tops up the net available funds (202) to give the net expenditure of 233 for the year. The net untouched / saved revenue at end of year 2 thus becomes 36.

(v)   ****47 = 36(saved the previous year) plus net income (11) during year 3 (179-168)

(vi)   *****: 187= previous year's savings (47) + net savings during year 4 (237-97=140);

(vii)   **Assumption**: Annual Interest rate on development loan = 18.75% p.a. (Compound); and Discount rate= 11%

18.0 TABLE 13: FINANCE VIII: NET INCOME PROJECTIONS, NET WORTH OF BUSINESS, FINANCIAL STABILITY AND SUSTAINABILITY OF PROJECT (IN 000 US$)
(ALL FIGURES DISCOUNTED TO THE PRESENT VALUE USING 11% DISCOUNT RATE)

END OF YEAR	1	2	3	4	5	6	7	8	9	10	11
Discounted net income	0	54	131	156	181	193	208	213	206	210	209
DISCOUNTED CUMMULATIVE INCOME (a)	0	54	185	341	522	715	923	1136	1342	1552	1761
DISCOUNTED EXPENDITURE	269	189	123	64	78	49	41	40	55	44	31
CUMMULATIVE DISCOUNTED EXPENDITURE (b)	269	458	471	535	613	662	703	743	798	842	873
Net worth (a-b)	-269	-404	-286	-194	-91	+53	180	393	544	710	888
COMMENT	Net loss	Net loss	Net loss	Net loss	Net loss	BREAKEVEN	NET PROFIT				

19.0: Figure 2: DISCOUNTED INCOME AND EXPENDITURE CHART (000US$)

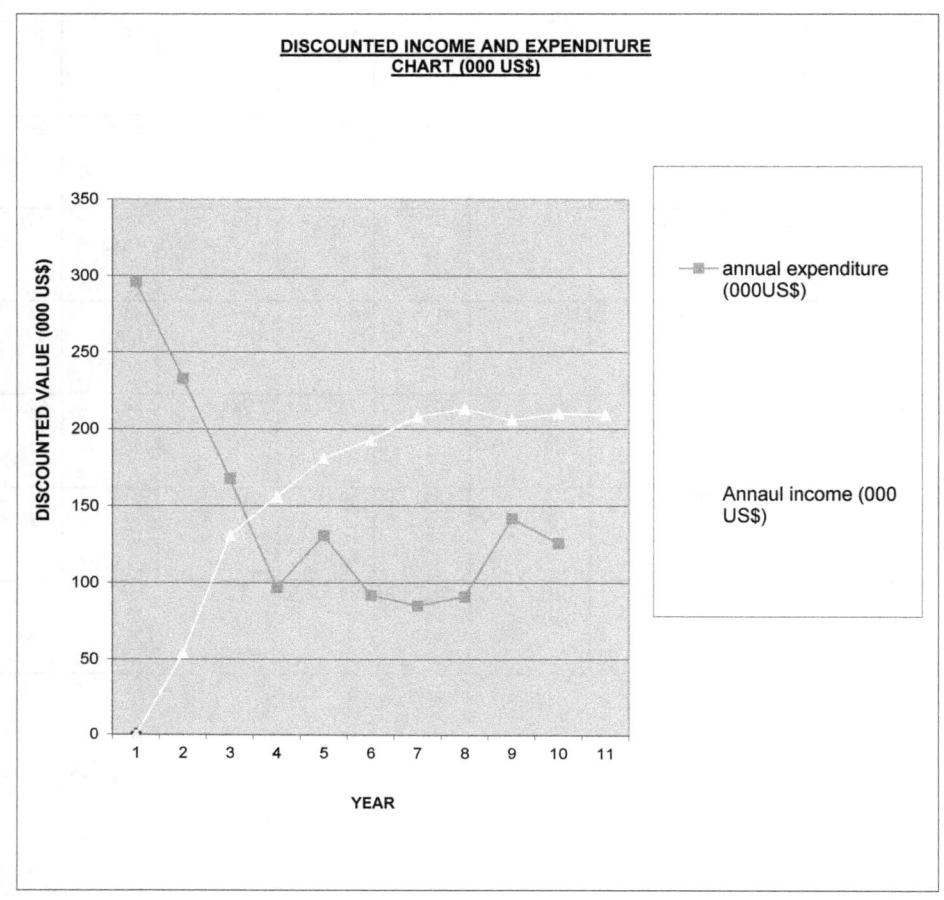

OTHERS
20.0   GAME POPULATION MANAGEMENT

This will be done as to suit the recommended carrying capacity of the land resource.

Culling will be done where the game exceed the carrying capacity, while extra protection will be given to those game deemed to be at risk. The culling will be accomplished by trophy hunting / shooting. This will be a major source of income to the project. The meat will then be sold to the willing buyers in different forms. Protection of endangered species will be done in zoos and other recommended methods. This will be a collaborative project among the community, the University partner and the XYZE.

20.1   PROJECT SIZE AND SUSTAINABILITY

According to Prof Verdoorn G (Endangered Wildlife trust, Game & hunting pp 43), large ranches can form ecologically sensible units where animals can move about freely, interact at their own will and sort out the fine balance that man still does not understand well. The term large could range from 10,000 – 50,000 ha depending on the ecological zone. Some farms have been as small as 3500 ha, yet very successful. Aim will be to improve the state of biodiversity in the region. It is on basis of this recommendation that we have chosen on the size of XYZE.

Focus is to have ecologically balanced farm whose benefits are huge but only reaped after a few years of sensible planning and management. Culling and hunting will be maximised just before the dry periods while the game are still in good enough condition to make them sell well but before they exhaust feed for the rest of the game. We hope to break even at the end of year 5 (i.e., during year 6)

20.2   **CONTRIBUTION TO NATIONAL AND INTERNATIONAL RESEARCH**

We will take a centre role in game research. We will establish game research laboratory in collaboration with our partners. We will also open our doors for learning by giving chance for attachment for research students in partner institutions. We will work hand in hand with wildlife clubs in schools and colleges to ensure the community benefits appropriately from the venture.

20.3   PARTNERSHIP AND COMMUNITY OUTREACH

We will strive to consolidate our strengths by pooling together our research resources with those of established institutions such as the University of Dar-es-salaam, and other Like-minded international institutions. Other than schools and college scouts, wildlife clubs and girl-guides, we will have a close partnership with the neighbouring community. We will have cultural tourism as our key venture, an activity in which community partnership is vital for its sustainability. In return, we plan to establish social amenities such as a school, a game-training institution and a clinic for use by the partner communities. Whereas we will have membership on payment, the partner communities will be automatic non- paying members.

20.4   ENVIRONMENTAL CARE, IMPACT ASSESSMEN AND MANAGEMENT

We will use the concept of primary environmental care (PEC) whereby environmental impacts will form the basis of our operation. At the onset, during the project survey, we will engage experts to conduct an EIA. Thereafter, there will be regular environmental audit. Lastly, other environmental aspects such as waste management will be well catered for by the construction of waste management facility. We initially propose to have waste stabilization ponds. For the solid wastes, we will liaise with the local authorities for approval of our proposed incinerator. As much as possible, we will strive to conserve energy by tapping energy from the incinerated wastes. On the energy part, we plan to utilise the solar power for all our undertakings. This has no environmental repercussions at all. Greening of the environment will be our key policy.

20.5   PROJECT EVALUATION

Besides a baseline survey to be done at the beginning of the project as part of planning to set benchmarks, We will have mini-evaluations (major monitoring activities) twice per year, and major evaluations every 2 years. The major ones will be conducted by a competent firm with proven records, and appointed by the management team. The evaluation report will form the basis of further development. The Management team will have a meeting to deliberate on the evaluation report, and thereafter, make new plans on how to progress.

20.6   MARKET RESEARCH AND INTELLIGENCE:

The will be conducted on regular basis to monitor opportunities, and trends of game farming and tourism, locally and internationally.

21   PROJECT REFEREES

....

TABLE 14: PHASED WORK PROGRAMME

PHASE	I		II		III		IV		V		OTHER
YEAR	1	2	3	4	5	6	7	8	9	10	11
EIA & EA		-	-	1	-	-	-	-	-	-	2
Market Survey	2	-	-	-	-	-	-	-	-	-	-
General survey	1										
Market research	1.0	2.0	2.0	2.0	2.0	2.0	2.0	2.0	2.0	2.0	2.0
Boundary demarcation & clearing)	1.2	-	-	-	-	-	-	-	-	-	-
Apiary construction	0.5	-	-	-	1.0	-	-	-	-	-	-
Botanical garden	2	2	2	-	-	2	-	-	-	-	-
Nature trail	5	2	5	-	-	5.0	-	-	-	-	-
Lodges	50	50	-	-	-	-	-	-	-	-	-
Tents for campsite	2	2	2	2	-	-	-	-	-	-	-
Campsite	5	5	3	3	-	-	-	-	-	-	-
Swimming pools	2	2	2	-	-	-	-	-	10	-	-
Aviary construction	1.0	-	-	-	-	-	-	-	-	-	-
Zoo construction	2.0	-	-	-	1.5	-	-	-	-	-	-
Dams (Game drinking)	5	5	5	-	5	-	-	-	-	-	-
Snake park construction	1	-	-	-	1.0	-	-	-	-	-	-
Resource centre	-	5	2	-	-	-	-	-	-	-	-
Frog ponds	1.0	-	-	-	-	-	-	-	-	-	-
Golf course	-	-	-	-	-	-	-	-	10	10	-
Fish ponds	1.0	-	-	-	1.5	-	-	-	1.5	-	-
Game proof fence	25.0	25.0	-	-	-	-	-	-	-	-	-
Research laboratories	-	10	10	-	-	-	-	-	-	-	-
Ordinary surveillance	-	5	5	5	5	5	5	5	5	5	5
Conference Complex	30	20	-	-	-	-	-	-	-	-	-
Conference facilities	10	5	5	5		-	-	-	-	-	-
Borehole drilling	5.4	1.8	-	-	-	-	-	-	-	-	-
Tents10@600$	6	-	-	-	-	-	-	-	-	-	-
Water distribution	2	1	1	1	-	-	-	-	-	--	-
Caravan	2	4	2	-	-	-	-	-	-	-	-
Water reservoirs	1.0	1.0	1.0	-	-	-	-	-	2	2	2
Recreational Park	2	2	2	-	-	-	-	-	-	-	-
Water tunnel (with splash pool)		5	5	-	-	-	-	-	10	-	-
Purchase of wildlife	20	20	20	10	10	-	-	-	-	-	-
Road Network	10	5	5	5	-	-	-	-	-	-	-
Solar canteen (cooking) (@ 1400$/80pple)	2.8	-	3.2	-	3.5	-	-	-	-	-	-
Photographic	5.0	1.0	1.0	1.0	1.0	1.0	1.0	1.0	1.0	1.0	1.0

equipment											
Waste management	2.0	2.0	2.0	2.0	2.0	2.0	2.0	2.0	2.0	2.0	2.0
Lighting / power supply	15	-	-	-	-	-	-	-	-	-	-
MARKETING											
Veterinary services	1.0	2.0	2.0	2.0	3.0	3.0	3.0	3.0	4.0	4.0	4.0
Environmental conservation	1.0	1.0	1.0	1.0	1.0	1.5	2.0	2.0	2.0	2.0	2.0
Staffing	10	15	20	25	30	35	40	40	40	40	40
Vehicles (4 WD)	24	-	30	-	30	-	-	-	15	15	-
General Mentenance	0.3	2.0	2.5	2.5	3.0	3.0	3.5	3.0	4.0	4.5	5.0
Establishment / offices	20	2	2	-	-	-	-	3.0	3.0	4.0	-
Project management	1	1	1	1	1	1	1	1	2	2	2

KEY

	HIGH LEVEL / HEAVY INVESTMENT
	MEDIUM LEVEL / MODERATE INVESTMENT
	LOW LEVEL / LIGHT INVESTMENT
	GENERAL MENTENANCE ONLY
	EXPANSION PHASE (LOAN REPAYMENT COMPLETE)
	RELY PARTLY ON INCOME GENERATED TO OPERATE
	100% RELIANCE ON LOAN / CONSTRUCTION PHASE
	FULL TIME LOAN PAYMENT YEARS
	BREAKEVEN YEAR
	LOAN PAYMENT BEGINS

TABLE 15: PLANNED TYPE AND NUMBERS OF GAME TO PURCHASE AND CULL (BY SHOOTING) (PRICES AND INCOME IN US$)

Game	Number to purchase	Unit price($)	TOTAL purchase cost	Hunting and shooting fee per animal (US$)	# of game hunted / yr	Total projected income from trophy hunting	Cummulative income from trophy hunting
Springbok	20	60	1,200	250	5	1250	1250
Blesbok	10	80	800	120	2	240	1490
Deer	10	30	300	150	4	600	2090
Eland	10	300	3,000	700	2	1400	3490
Kudu	10	180	1,800	700	3	2100	5590
Gemsbok	10	400	4,000	400	3	1200	6790
Black wildebeest	5	100	500	300	2	600	7390
Red hartebeest	10	200	2,000	350	2	700	8090
Eland Female	8	400	3,200	600	1	600	8690
Zebra	8	250	2,000	420	2	840	9530
Nyala	5	700	3,500	1,000	2	2000	11,530
Waterbuck	8	450	3,600	650	2	1300	12,830
Lion	5	1200	6,000	5,000	2	10,000	22,830
Leopard	6	900	5,400	3,000	2	6,000	28,830
Giraffe	8	1000	8,000	3,000	2	6,000	34,830
TOTAL			45,300				34,830

Carrying capacity calculations will be based on the Meisner tables and the mentis tables

24   APPENDIX III: PARTICULARS OF APPLICANT

1   **PERSONAL DETAILS**

Names:

Address: SUSTAINABLE   FUTURES,   P.O.   BOX   21869,   MAUN,
BOTSWANA.

Cell: **267-71517548**

Fax: 267- 6863896

E-mail:

Nationality: Tanzanian

2   **ACADEMIC AND PROFESSIONAL QUALIFICATIONS**

Degree	Institution	Year
MSc (Agriculture) (Agronomy & farming systems)	University of Adelaide, South Australia	1998
BSc (Agriculture)	Sokoine University, Morogoro, Tanzania	1994
Post-graduate certificate in Production, evaluation and utilisation of food legumes	Kasetsart University, Bangkok, Thailand	1996
Foundation certificate in health & safety	Chartered Institute of Environmental Health, UK	2001

3   **WORK EXPERIENCE:**

Institution and location	Position	From	To
Sustainable Futures, Botswana	Director-Research & Publishing	March 2003	Date
Afullo & Associates Consultancy & Training Firm, Botswana	Trainer in Agricultural hazard analyst, risk assessor & coordinator	Jan 2001	March 2003
WEDC & Loughborough University, UK	Academic advisor in an MSc distance learning programme	Nov 2002	Date
Mlingano Agricultural Research & Training Institute, Ministry of Agriculture, Tanzania	Research Officer	July 1994	1999
Mlingano Agricultural Research & Training Institute, Ministry of Agriculture, Tanzania	Part-time Lecturer in agriculture (Diploma in crop science students)	July 1994	1999

4   **CURRENT & FUTURE ACTIVITIES**

Current activity	Institution	Dates
Academic advisor	Loughborough University & WEDC, UK	2002-2006
Research	Sustainable futures	20003-
Research & PublishingDirector	Sustainable futures	**2003-**
DIRECTOR	XYZ ECOTOURISM FARM	**2004-**

5   REFEREES

25. REFERENCES

1. Farmers' weekly October 2003. pp 35-36

2. Farmers weekly, pp 31, August 2002

3. Game & Hinting 2003 August)

Notes:

An animal in captivity meant for hunting should be released at least 24 hours before the hunt, and the animal may not be hunted in a camp smaller than 1000 ha, and this area must be approved by the right department.. breeders may not permit hunting on the same farm. (Farmers weekly, pp 31, August 2002)